Calling All Saints

Calling All Saints

Brother T.N. Costa

Troitsa Books
Commack, NY

Editorial Production: Susan Boriotti
Assistant Vice President/Art Director: Maria Ester Hawrys
Office Manager: Annette Hellinger
Graphics: Frank Grucci
Acquisitions Editor: Tatiana Shohov
Book Production: Ludmila Kwartiroff, Christine Mathosian,
   Joanne Metal and Tammy Sauter
Circulation: Iyatunde Abdullah, Cathy DeGregory, and Maryanne Schmidt

Library of Congress Cataloging-in-Publication Data

Tom-Nicholas, Brother.
   Calling all saints/ by Brother Tom-Nicholas.
   p. cm.
   ISBN 1-56072-534-6
   1. Christian saints-- Biography.- 2. Christian saints--Meditations.
   I. Title.
   BX4657.T64 1997
   270'.092'2--dc21   97-45678
   [B]   CIP

Copyright © 1998 by Tom-Nicholas, Brother
   Troitsa Books. A division of
   Nova Science Publishers, Inc.
   6080 Jericho Turnpike, Suite 207
   Commack, New York 11725
   Tele. 516-499-3103   Fax 516-499-3146
   E Mail Novascience@earthlink.net
   Web Site: http://www.nexusworld.com/nova

All rights reserved. No part of this book may be reproduced, stored in a retrieval system or transmitted in any form or by any means: electronic, electrostatic, magnetic, tape, mechanical, photocopying, recording or otherwise without permission from the publishers.

The authors and publisher haven taken care in preparation of this book, but make no expressed or implied warranty of any kind and assume no responsibility for any errors or omissions. No liability is assumed for incidental or consequential damages in connection with or arising out of information contained in this book.

This publication is designed to provide accurate and authoritative information with regard to the subject matter covered herein. It is sold with the clear understanding that the publisher is not engaged in rendering legal or any other professional services. If legal or any other expert assistance is required, the services of a competent person should be sought. FROM A DECLARATION OF PARTICIPANTS JOINTLY ADOPTED BY A COMMITTEE OF THE AMERICAN BAR ASSOCIATION AND A COMMITTEE OF PUBLISHERS.

Printed in the United States of America

DEDICATION

To Rev. Peter C. Ensor,
the Godfather of St. James' Church

Contents

Dedication v
Ita 1
Francis de Sales 3
John Bosco 5
Brigid of Ireland 7
Jerome Emiliani 9
Valentine 11
David of Wales 13
Patrick 15
Joseph 17
Damien of Molokai 19
George 23
Catherine of Sienna 25
Monica 27
Pachomius 29
Isidore the Farmer 31
Joan of Arc 33
Kevin 35
Barnabas 37
Anthony of Padua 35
Peter 41
Elizabeth of Portugal 43
Camillus 45
Bonaventure 47
Mary Magdalene 49
John Vianney 51
Dominic 53

Clare of Assisi	55
Fiacre	57
Hildegard of Bingen	59
Matthew	61
Francis of Assisi	63
Francis Borgia	65
John of Capistrano	67
Martin de Porres	69
Charles Borromeo	71
Margaret of Scotland	73
Elizabeth of Hungary	75
John of Damascus	77
Nicholas	79
Thomas the Apostle	81

ITA
JANUARY 15

Ita is considered the second greatest woman saint in Ireland, right after St. Brigid. She is also known as Ida and Mida, although her baptismal name was actually Deirdre, and she was born of royal descent near County Waterford.

Several noble suitors wanted to marry her, but she refused them all. Through prayers, speeches, and, according to legend, some angelic assistance, her father finally agreed to let her become a nun. She moved to Limerick and attracted enough woman followers to start her own religious order. Their main Christian service was to run a grammar school for boys, at the request of St. Ere, the local bishop. This gives Sister Ita the reputation of starting the first parochial school in Ireland.

One famous student grew up to become St. Brendan of Ireland. He was taught by Ita for 5 years when he was a young boy. Brendan later wrote in his memoirs that his childhood teacher was one of the greatest influences for good in his life.

Which brings us to the Christian idea of mentorship. We've all seen those public service announcements on television, the mini-commercials where a famous actor or actress tells how a teacher in their past inspired them to do more. Christ's command to love God and love one another can also be seen as a command to teach, to affirm, and to motivate one another to do good. That's why teaching is such a noble profession: helping people, young or old, to learn new ideas and explore new dreams and new worlds of imagination and knowledge. When Ita decided to dedicate her life to teaching, she sought to change the world around her for the better, one student at a time.

So never miss a chance to be a teacher, a mentor, a coach, or a role model, whether for adults or for children. And say a prayer for all the teachers in your life who, like Saint Ita, inspired you to go for the gold.

FRANCIS DE SALES
JANUARY 24

Francis was born a member of the French nobility in 1567. He wanted to be a priest at an early age, but to please his father he went to the University of Paris and studied law as well as theology. After graduating from law school at age 24, he finally convinced his father that he still had the dream of becoming a priest. He was ordained two years later, but only after his father got him a cushy job working for the Bishop of Geneva.

Francis volunteered for the work of bringing people who were disillusioned with religion back to Christ. He looked for new ways to reach the man in the street, and began writing leaflets and booklets explaining different religious ideas in simple language. This was the start of a very successful writing career. He eventually became so famous that the Pope made Francis the Bishop of Geneva 10 years later.

Francis was a firm believer in the need for Christian education for children, and he organized classes for them throughout his diocese. He was well-known for his charity and kindness, and was loving, but firm, with those who were on the wrong path.

He also dealt with the issue of whether having wealth was a deterrent to being a good Christian. In his spiritual best-seller, ***Introduction to the Devout Life***, Francis wrote, "There is a difference between having poison and being poisoned." He pointed out that pharmacists keep all kinds of potentially dangerous drugs on hand, but they aren't poisoning themselves because the drugs are in their shops, not in their bodies. Francis reasoned that as long as our wealth is used for good things instead of selfish ones, it won't necessarily corrupt us.

One of the dangers of possessions is how quickly and easily they can possess us. We've got a fancy food processor at home and it works great, but did you ever experience the hassle of trying to clean one? We all know people who save every Christmas and birthday present because "they're just too nice to use." My mom was that way with the good dishes and towels. They were just "for company," resulting in tons of beautiful, unused things crammed in the linen closet and china cabinet, until the day she died.

St. Francis de Sales would say that the things of this life are here for us to appreciate and share. It is only when we use our God-given possessions and talents for the good of others that they will contribute to our own happiness and well-being. So perhaps now is the time to think about sharing some of your talents, financial and otherwise, both with those you love, and with those in need of love.

And, oh yes, start using some of those good towels today!

JOHN BOSCO
JANUARY 31

He was born in 1815, the youngest son of a peasant farmer who died when John was 2. He had to work at various odd jobs as soon as he was old enough to make money to help out his family. In his spare time he became an accomplished magician and acrobat, and would put on shows before church in the marketplace. After taking his bows, young John would lead his audience into church to attend Mass.

He decided he really wanted to become a priest, and entered the seminary when he was 16. His family could not afford to buy him the required wardrobe, so all his seminary clothes had to be donated. The mayor gave him a hat, his parish priest donated a cloak, one parishioner bought him his cassock, while another bought John his first pair of shoes.

After he was ordained in 1841, Father John (or "Don Bosco" as he was called in Italy) decided to make his life's work the education of disadvantaged boys, sort of like Father Flanagan and "Boys Town." With his outgoing personality, he easily made friends with several wealthy benefactors in the area who provided funds for his youth work. He started taking in homeless boys, and before long Don Bosco and his mother (better known as "Mamma Margaret") were running a boardinghouse for 40 boys at the rectory. The boys went out to work each morning and then came back home at suppertime. John realized he could give the boys a Christian education if he could train them to earn a living at home, so in 1853 he opened two vocational schools to teach shoemaking and tailoring.

He built a new parish church named after his favorite saint, St. Francis de Sales, and founded a religious order of priests, called the Salesians, to assist him in his work. Three years later he and 10 other priests were teaching 150 boys in a boarding school residence, with 500 more boys as day students in four different vocational schools.

In 1872 John realized he couldn't overlook the chance of helping poor girls. He founded an order of nuns called the "Daughters of Our Lady, Help of Christians," and they started similar schools for girls in Italy, Brazil, and Argentina. He was well known as a eloquent speaker and made several speaking tours throughout Italy to raise money for his various educational projects. By the time of his death in 1888, his two religious orders had established 64 schools worldwide.

John Bosco was a firm believer in the concept: "Give someone a fish and they'll eat for a day; teach them to fish and they'll eat for a lifetime." He saw the way to get his boys out of poverty was to train them to get jobs. He wanted to give them a hand, not a handout.

Sometimes true love means challenging those in our care to do better, to reach higher, to change and to grow. Like St. John, the former magician, we all can use the power of love to give others the confidence to change their fearful, "I can't" to those magic words, "Yes, I can!"

BRIGID OF IRELAND
FEBRUARY 1

Also known as St. Bride, Brigid was born in Ireland in 450. One legend says her father was a Irish king. Another tradition is that he was a dairy farmer, and Brigid had to help out with the cows when she was young, which might explain how she became the patron saint of dairy-workers and milkmen. She is the Patroness of Ireland as well, giving her the number two spot after St. Patrick.

She decided to become a nun at an early age. Later she founded the first convent in Ireland in the town of Kildare that become a great center of learning. St. Brigid also founded an art school where the students learned to do illuminated manuscripts.

It was said that she was so humble that she blushed every time she had to speak to someone, and that her main desire in life was to satisfy the hunger of the poor, expel every hardship, and spare every unhappy person from the sorrows of this world.

One legend of her kindness and hospitality tells how she and her nuns spent a long day feeding the poor by giving away every loaf of bread, every egg, and every piece of fruit in the convent kitchen. Suddenly word came that a delegation of seven bishops were on their way to pay St. Brigid a visit. The other nuns were frantic because they had nothing left to prepare a meal for such important guests.

Mother Superior Brigid simply said, "Go forth and ask the hens to kindly lay more eggs. Speak to the trees and see what fruit they have left, and talk gently to the cows and beg them for a little more milk." She herself went to start the fire in the oven, but when she opened it, there appeared 12 loaves of hot baked bread. The hens laid more eggs, the cows gave milk, and apples and pears fell from the trees into the nuns' aprons. And the bishops that evening vowed that they had never sat down to a more magnificent feast!

Well, maybe it didn't exactly happen like that, but the moral of the story is that Brigid's great faith that Christ would "give us this day our daily bread" is what really made that mealtime miracle. And like St. Brigid, by giving of ourselves through love we receive far more than we could ever ask or imagine. Her life shows us that it truly is better to give than to receive. And having a few of those magic chickens certainly couldn't hurt.

JEROME EMILIANI
FEBRUARY 8

Jerome was born in Venice, Italy in 1481, and became an officer in the Venetian army. He led a typical tough-guy soldier's life with not much use for prayers and for God. That is until he was taken prisoner in a battle and chained up in a dungeon. All of a sudden, he was literally stuck. To his credit, he used his imprisonment to consider his options and reevaluated his life. Once free, he left the military to enter the priesthood at age 37, and decided to work at relieving the famine and plague that was devastating northern Italy at the time.

When he himself caught, and then recovered from, the plague in 1531, Jerome devoted the rest of his life to the care of others. First on his to-do list was taking care of all the children who had been orphaned because of the plague. He bought a house, fed and clothed the orphans at his own expense, and gave them a Christian education. Jerome ended up founding a total of three orphanages plus a hospital. The one-time soldier of fortune became a model of sanctity, and even ended up becoming the patron saint of orphans.

St. Jerome realized that what sometimes seems to be a dead end is actually a doorway in disguise. But in order to discover that door, we have to be willing to take a chance and open our eyes, our minds, and our hearts to its existence. There's also an old saying that when God shuts a door in our lives, He always opens a window.

So what should we do when we're at a dead-end in our daily life, be it physical or spiritual? Follow the lead of St. Jerome and learn to open our eyes to God's new possibilities for us.

VALENTINE
FEBRUARY 14

There really was a St. Valentine...and maybe even two. One was a priest, the other a bishop, and both were martyred in Rome on February 14 according to the ***Roman Martyrology***, an early catalogue of Christian martyrs. Since their stories and legends are so similar, it's quite possible that both were one and the same person.

One legend says a Roman priest named Valentine assisted the Christians who were being persecuted during the time of the Emperor Claudius II. Valentine was arrested, imprisoned, and later beheaded outside the gates of Rome on February 14. According to another version of the story, the Emperor had forbidden young men in the Roman legions to marry, because he thought single men made better soldiers. Father Valentine did not agree, so he secretly married several young couples who came to him for help. Upon hearing this, the Emperor declared that no one, not even a Christian priest, could defy an Imperial order, so he threw Valentine into prison.

Another story says that while awaiting execution, Bishop Valentine converted his jailer's daughter to Christianity after he cured her blindness. He wrote her a series of instructive letters signed: "From your Valentine." Still another legend relates how St. Valentine made friends with many children. The Romans imprisoned him because he refused to worship their gods. The children missed Valentine and tossed notes of love and hope between the bars of his cell, giving us the custom of sending Valentine cards on his feastday.

Pope Julius I built a church over the tomb of Valentine the Martyr, and in 496 Pope Gelasius named February 14th as St. Valentine's feastday. This gradually became known as a special day for exchanging love letters, and St. Valentine ended up as the patron saint of courtship and lovers. He also has one of the few feastdays that is still an official holiday on our modern calendars (St. Patrick's Day is the only other one that comes to mind).

Even though the stories and legends don't always agree, it's nice to know there's a patron saint to remind us to spend at least one day a year celebrating the joys and simple pleasures of flowers, boxes of chocolates, and greeting cards to publicly express our love and devotion. St. Valentine lived the words of Christ: "Love one another as I have loved you."

So go ahead: tell someone, "I love you" today. And to play it safe, you better pick up that box of candy as well. St. Valentines' Day is no time to take chances with love.

DAVID OF WALES
MARCH 1

Born the son of a Welsh chieftain in 520, St. David became famous as a preacher, holy man, and miracle worker. He is the patron saint of Wales, and the only Welsh saint to be widely recognized in the Western Church. He founded his first monastery at Mynyw in the southwest corner of the country. He eventually founded 11 others as well, including Glastonbury Abbey in western England, where legend has it King Arthur and Queen Guineviere of Camelot fame are buried.

His monastic rule was very strict, and modeled on the way of life of the desert-hermit monks of the early Church. Hard, manual labor was the rule for all monks, and they were not allowed to keep oxen or horses to use in plowing the fields. The only food allowed was vegetables, bread, and salt. The only drink permitted was water, sometimes mixed with a little milk, giving St. David the nickname in medieval records of "David the Waterman."

He was asked to attend a synod in Cardigan, and was said to have spoken with such wisdom and eloquence that he was unanimously elected the Head Bishop (or Primate) of Wales, since the position just happened to be available.

It has been said that his last words to his monks were, "Keep your faith, and do the little things you have seen and done with me." St. David believed that it wasn't the once-in-a-lifetime events and accomplishments that bring us closer to Christ, but simple, everyday acts of kindness. Little things, done with much love, can be the greatest gift of all.

PATRICK
MARCH 17

On March 17, everybody, regardless of national origin, can be a little Irish. For someone whose life contains as much fiction as fact, St. Patrick is still one of the most famous saints of all time. Although St. Patrick's Day is best known for shamrocks, leprechauns, and everything being green (including the beer), it's really a celebration of St. Patrick's missionary efforts that brought Christianity to 5th Century Ireland.

He was born in Britain of a Christian family. In fact his father was a deacon and his grandfather was a priest (this was before the days of mandatory celibacy for the priesthood). When he was about 14 years old, Patrick was captured by a Saxon raiding party. He was sold into slavery and shipped off to Ireland where he had to work as a shepherd.

Seven years later, Patrick escaped, got passage on a ship, and made it back home to his family in Britain. But by this time he had a dream: to become a priest and return to Ireland as a missionary. His family was totally against it, but no one could dissuade him. Patrick was ordained and returned to Ireland, accompanied by 20 priests and deacons to set up churches and missions. Due to his determination and great abilities, it wasn't long before Patrick was consecrated as the first Archbishop of Ireland.

Besides setting up churches and abbeys (and doing legendary things like driving snakes out of the Emerald Isle), St. Patrick is also believed to have written the prayer entitled "The Breastplate of St. Patrick." Also known as Hymn No. 370 in the Episcopal Church Hymnbook, this is a song they often use at the ordinations of priests and deacons:

"Christ be with me, Christ before me,

> Christ behind me, Christ beneath me....
> Christ in quiet and in danger,
> Christ in hearts of all that love me,
> Christ in mouth of friend and stranger...."

Although we can't be absolutely certain St. Patrick is the author, this ancient prayer is a perfect reflection of his life and beliefs. Everything he did was out of a passionate belief in Christ's message of love. At a time when few people could read and write, St. Patrick's life became a living Gospel for all to see.

And if it's true that we are what we eat, it follows that our lives will reflect what we truly believe. If we follow the gospel of materialism and self-interest, that will be apparent to all we meet. But if we, like St. Patrick, embrace the true Gospel of love and service for others, we can become messengers and missionaries of life and love and hope for a lonely world.

And that's no blarney!

JOSEPH
MARCH 19

St. Joseph was a carpenter, a skilled professional who was a respected and necessary member of his community. He was obviously good at his job, and he would have taught Jesus the trade as well.

This isn't to say that Joseph and the Holy Family were well-off financially. They weren't. In Jesus' time, you were in one of three classes: the wealthy nobility or rich merchant class on one end; a beggar, leper or other "untouchable" on the other end; and everyone else would be in the middle, working hard to earn a living and keep a roof over their heads. Jesus, Mary and Joseph would have been no exception.

Another thing is that St. Joseph had to pack up and relocate his family several times, whether or not he was ready to do so. The first time was when he had to leave Nazareth with Mary to register for the census in Bethlehem. The Gospels seem to imply that they lived there for a while before Joseph had to relocate again to move the family to Egypt to get away from King Herod. He obviously had to set up another carpentry business from scratch in Egypt until he had another dream saying it was safe to go back to Nazareth. Most of these moves had to do with God's mission for St. Joseph and his family. And that's probably how he got the job of Patron Saint of House-Hunting. He must have been a great "Home Improvement" kind of guy for Mary to have around. You need a real professional to turn a stable into a home. Of course it probably helps if you have assorted kings and/or wise men stopping by with expensive housewarming gifts.

Scripture says St. Joseph was "a good and just man." Nothing fancy, no high office, just a hard-working guy taking care of the wife and kids. I suppose St. Joseph would tell us that the goal in life is to do the best we can, and then trust in God to take care of the rest. And don't forget to measure twice before you cut that 2 x 4.

DAMIEN OF MOLOKAI
APRIL 15

Damien de Veuster was born in Belgium in 1840. He decided that he wanted the adventure of being a missionary to far-off lands, so he joined the Fathers of the Sacred Heart, became a priest, and then received permission to set sail for the Hawaiian Islands in 1863. After a voyage that lasted five months, he arrived in Honolulu and was assigned to a mission on the neighboring island of Maui, where he worked for the next 10 years.

In the late 1800s the Hawaiian Islands suffered a severe outbreak of leprosy. Leprosy and other diseases like measles and tuberculosis had never existed in Hawaii until foreign traders arrived, decimating the native population in the process. The influential American and British businessmen were so terrified by the leprosy epidemic that they pressured the government of King Kamehameha V to force all lepers to report to government doctors for inspection and final banishment to the island of Molokai. Anyone who refused was to be shot.

When the medical inspectors and soldiers arrived on Maui, Father Damien saw whole families, along with their stricken sons, daughters, and parents, come to his church on their knees, all begging the good *Kahuna* (Hawaiian for priest) to plead with the officials to let them nurse their loved ones at home for the few months or years that remained. But despite his best efforts, the government orders were carried out without exception. Father Damien never forgot the agonizing cries and tears of the Hawaiian families being torn apart forever because of the disease brought to them by outsiders.

A few months later when the Bishop of Hawaii asked for a missionary to volunteer to serve the lepers, Father Damien signed up without a second thought, knowing full well he would have to remain on Molokai forever.

Life at the leper colony was a death sentence of suffering and despair. The crews in the supply boats were afraid to land, so they would row in close, then force the lepers to jump overboard and swim to shore as best as they could. Those who made it found a prison without law and order, full of desperate men and women, with the strong preying on the weak.

Father Damien decided from the start to bring order and compassion to the chaos of the sick and dying. He organized burial details and funeral services. He taught and motivated the people to grow crops and feed themselves better. He designed an irrigation system, houses, even a new church, and everyone who was strong enough pitched in to help.

He also gave his flock continual medical attention. Doctors visited the colony on a semi-regular basis but they were afraid to touch the lepers. They would inspect the patients from a distance, then leave medicines and instructions with Father Damien, who would do the actual hands-on treatment of his congregation.

Then the day came in 1885 when Damien realized he had the first symptoms of the dreaded disease. Although he had labored for 25 years in relative obscurity, once the news broke of the brave priest becoming a leper, editors of newspapers and weekly magazines found him sensational copy. The story of his illness was telegraphed around the world, and in a matter of weeks millions of people learned about Father Damien and the tragedy of the Hawaiian lepers.

A small group of volunteers came to help, inspired by Damien's story. First two priests arrived, and then 2 lay-brothers: Brother James from Australia, and Brother Joseph Dutton, a former Civil War medical officer from Boston. Three Franciscan nuns also came from Honolulu with supplies and equipment to set up a hospital. Donations started pouring into Molokai from around the world. Robert Louis Stevenson, who was visiting in Hawaii, described the feeling of the time when he wrote: "Father Damien is my father...and the father of all who love goodness; he is your father, too, if God has given you the grace to see it."

Although a new drug treatment for leprosy had been discovered in Europe, it came too late for the good Kahuna. Father Damien continued to work with the congregation he loved until his death on April 15, 1889.

And what is the message of this sad love story? I believe it's that no matter the pestilence of a particular age, be it leprosy, polio, or AIDS, human love and compassion will always shine forth, even in the darkest hours. Father Damien saw what others considered a hopeless and lost cause, and by his faith made everyone he touched a better person. Even 100 years later, that love which surpasses all understanding touches us still. His life shows us that it's always better to light one small candle of hope than to curse the darkness of this world. "For these three last forever: faith, hope, and love; but the greatest of these... is love."

GEORGE
APRIL 23

St. George has been the patron saint of soldiers for nearly a thousand years. He was a solder himself, and was martyred for the faith during the persecution carried out by the Roman Emperor Diocletian in the early 4th century. But it is the legend of his brave confrontation with a dragon that made him famous.

The story goes that he rode into a town in Asia Minor which was being terrorized by a dragon that lived in a swamp on the outskirts of the town. The people had gotten together to try to kill it, but the dragon's breath (fire-breathing and otherwise) was so bad that they gave up that idea. To appease the dragon, they supplied him with 2 sheep per day for breakfast.

When sheep grew scarce, human sacrifices were chosen by lot, one of which fell to the ruler's daughter. She dressed herself as a bride and rode out to meet her doom, whereupon St. George appeared and attacked the dragon with his lance. He tied up the wounded beast and dragged him into town, promising to slay the dragon if the people converted to Christianity. Under the circumstances, the whole town flocked to be baptized, and St. George dispatched the dragon.

His fame through this legend spread rapidly, and it was written down so many times that it gradually began to have a ring of truth about it. Over the centuries, soldiers have looked to him as the perfect example of bravery in battle, and he became their patron saint. St. George was called upon to lend his weight to the Crusaders' side in there war against the Saracens in the 13th century. After a vision of St. George appeared to Richard the Lionhearted's armies at the siege of Antioch, he declared him patron saint of England.

St. George was probably just a hard-working soldier turned Christian martyr who would be amazed and probably embarrassed to think that we only remember him as a first-class dragon-slayer. But even St. George would admit that, with faith in God, there's lots of personal dragons we can all slay: Fear, Doubt, Loneliness, Not-Wanting-To-Get-Involved....all the great dragons of modern life that try to keep us from reaching out to the love of Christ and to one another. St. George would tell us that it was his faith in God that killed that dragon in the swamp. Well, maybe that and a good suit of shining, fire-proof armor.

CATHERINE OF SIENNA
APRIL 29

Catherine was born in Sienna, Italy in 1347, the youngest of 25 children. Her father was a well-to do cloth merchant and dyer. At the age of 12 she decided she wanted to become a nun and never marry. This greatly angered her parents, since a good match could bring social position and financial gain to the rising merchant class. Her parents tried everything to change her mind, finally forcing her to do all the menial tasks in the house, like scrubbing floors, washing dishes, doing all the laundry, and refusing to let her to read books or have any time by herself....sort of an Italian version of Cinderella. Finally her father gave up, and she was allowed to join the Dominican Third Order for lay people.

She spent the next few years in prayer and study, only leaving her room to go to church. But then Catherine had one of several visions of Christ and the Virgin Mary who told her she must now go forth into the world and see to the salvation of her neighbors. She gradually left her room and starting meeting people again. Soon she had a regular group of friends, relatives, and townspeople coming to see her for advice and spiritual direction, and it wasn't longer before they all joined the Third Order, with Catherine as spiritual director of the group. She called them her "fellowship-family", and they called her "Mama Catherine."

Because of her reputation for healing family feuds, she was often called upon to mediate business, religious, and political disputes. This was the era of continual wars and power struggles between the various city-states of Europe. She wrote letters and made personal visits to dukes and barons in Italy, France and Germany to bring warring factions to the peace table in the name of Christ. She was the personal friend and confidante of two popes, Gregory XI and Urban VI. After being elected Pope, Urban let the honor go to his head, and became arrogant, abrasive and tyrannical. The cardinals met again in France and declared the first election to have been held under duress and, therefore, invalid. They elected a new Pope, Clement VII, who took up residence in Avignon, France. Catherine worked overtime on the problem, both to persuade Urban to mend his ways, and to persuade other leaders that the peace and unity of the Church demanded the recognition of Urban as the one true Pope. Through her continual efforts she respectfully but firmly showed Pope Urban the error of his ways, causing some historians of the time to remark that "Sister Catherine has perfected the art of kissing the Pope's feet while simultaneously twisting his arm."

While all this was going on, she found time to write a collection of four books on the spiritual life, known as the "Dialogues of St. Catherine." All this before she died at the age of 33.

She lived her life with a strong faith in the power of prayer, and the need for activism, counseling, and love. Above all, she lived Christ's message of "blessed are the peacemakers," and believed that peace among cities and nations would only come if peace started at home with every family. Problems between siblings, parents who refuse to speak to a certain grownup son or daughter, long-lost friends who can't forgive and forget a hurt from the past: these are all reasons to stop and consider the example of St. Catherine. Be the first to reach out and mend those broken fences. Pick up the phone, write that letter, and make that visit. St. Catherine would say that it's the Christ-like thing to do. And you better believe that when it comes to peacemaking, Mama Catherine knows best.

MONICA
MAY 4

St. Monica was a woman who had it all: an angry husband, a bad-tempered mother-in-law, and a very smart but immoral son who much later became St. Augustine. In spite of the aggravations of her family, Monica became a saint and helped her son to become one as well.

No matter how difficult things were at home, St. Monica was always patient and kind to everyone, and she prayed constantly for her husband and son to change. After many years, her husband finally followed her example and became a Christian before he died. But not her son, Augustine. From the age of 18 when he went away to college, Augustine lived a life of wine, women and song both in North Africa and later in Rome where he moved with his mistress and illegitimate son to start his own school. He taught courses in rhetoric and public speaking to the sons of the Roman nobility.

St. Monica eventually followed him to Rome, and never gave up on him or her faith in God to turn him around. Finally after, get this: 17 years of prayers, Augustine saw the error of his ways, was baptized at age 33, and eventually became one of the greatest bishops and theologians of the Church.

St. Monica did not became famous just because of her son. She was a saint in her own right because of her patience, her persistence, and her great faith that Christ is truly present in each one of us. She never gave up, which is the moral of today's story. So many of us expect our prayers to be answered instantly, the way we get instant coffee, microwave pizza, and 100 channels of cable television at the touch of a remote button. But God does not always answer in a instant. He handles things in His time frame, not ours. Faith is really a long-term goal, a daily conversion to turn away from sin and reach out to Christ. St. Monica was right on target when it came to prayer and to making a difference in someone's life: be patient, be persistent, and don't ever give up.

PACHOMIUS
MAY 9

He was born in Egypt in 292, and was drafted by force into the army of the Emperor at age 20. When he and the other recruits (more like galley slaves, actually) were being conveyed down the Nile, they received great kindness from Christians at the city of Latopolis, who were moved with compassion for them.

Pachomius never forgot the Christian charity given to him, a total stranger, so as soon as his tour of duty was over, he made his way back home and started studying to become a Christian himself. After he was baptized, he decided to devote his life to prayer and meditation, so be begged a famous local hermit named Paloemon, who lived in the desert, to teach him how to be a good desert-hermit monk. The two of them ate only bread and water, and spent all day and most of the night in prayer and manual labor. It appears Paloemon was something of a 4th century building contractor, and he taught his young disciple all he knew about stone and brickwork.

Pachomius put this new knowledge to good use when he helped design and build a monastery along the banks of the Nile after several other men asked to join him, including his eldest brother, John. It wasn't long before there were 100 monks following Pachomius' "Rules For Monastic Life," which was something of a spiritual bestseller in Egypt at the time. He established six other monasteries in Egypt, and built a church for poor shepherds near Thebes. He served as a lector at that church, but could never to induced to become a priest, nor would he allow any of his monks to become ordained, feeling that their vocation was a different kind of calling from God.

He also built a convent across the Nile for his sister and a group of nuns that wanted to follow his monastic rules. Legend has it he could walk among the snakes and scorpions in the desert and never get bitten. It was also said that whenever he wanted to cross the Nile River to visit his sister, Pachomius had his own special version of monk mass-transit: crocodiles would show up to carry him across and set him down wherever he liked.

"Look at the Christians...see how they love one another!" was how one Roman historian admiringly described the early Christians. What to Pachomius seemed a random act of kindness from total strangers became the spark of love that changed his whole way of thinking and led him to a new way of life.

Why not do the same for someone today? Try showing a little more love and understanding to someone who could use a smile and a kind word. Who knows? The life you change could be your own.

ISIDORE THE FARMER
MAY 15

The patron saint of farmers was born in Spain of poor parents. As soon as he was old enough, Isidore signed on as a farmworker on a wealthy landowner's estate outside the city of Madrid. He stayed with that one employer, and that one job, for the rest of his life.

Isidore combined a great love for God and his fellow man with a great love for the land. He would dedicate his daily work in the fields to God, and was generous to those poorer than himself, often sharing his meals with them. He also had a great love for animals, putting him in the good company of St. Francis and St. Kevin.

One winter's day as he and another farm-hand were taking sacks of corn to the mill, Isidore noticed a flock of birds perched in the barren tree branches, obviously cold and hungry and unable to find any food in the frost-covered ground. Over the jeers of his companion, Isidore opened his sack and poured half of the corn on the ground for the birds. When the two men finally reached the mill, Isidore's sack was found to be completely full, and after grinding, produced twice a much cornmeal as usual.

"*Laborare est orare*" ("to labor is to pray") was an idea first conceived by St. Benedict when he set up a rule of life for the monks in his monasteries. The idea was that manual labor should be considered a good and holy thing, and just as important as time spent in prayer and meditation. Isidore would pray as he plowed, because he knew that being the best farmer he could be was his way to give glory to God.

All of our talents and skills, and all forms of work can be considered great gifts. It's simply how we look at them. You can think of your job as monotonous drudgery, or you can see it as a service to others. It can be an endless, stressful ordeal, or it can be a prayer of thanksgiving for the simple gifts of this life. It's really just a question of attitude.

So whether we work behind a plow like St. Isidore or work behind a computer; whether we're changing tires or just changing diapers; we can use the simple tasks of daily life to bring us all closer to the love of Christ.

JOAN OF ARC
MAY 30

Joan was just another French country girl until, at age 14, she started hearing the voices of St. Michael the Archangel, St. Catherine of Alexandria, and St. Margaret of Antioch. At age 16 they had convinced Joan that she was to rescue the City of Orleans from the English and re-establish the Dauphin of France to the throne. Charles, the Dauphin, was next in line to be king, but his coronation had been postponed because of the war.

She went to see the commander of the French forces in a nearby town and offered her services, but the commander just laughed at her. But when the same commander suffered a major defeat as predicted by Joan, he called her back and sent her to meet the Dauphin, accompanied by his personal military escort.

She was forced to wait around for 3 weeks, because most of the royal court considered her either a crazy girl or an English spy. Only after a group of theologians gave Joan their seal of approval was she allowed to see Charles, who gave her command of an army to try to re-take the City of Orleans. Wearing a special custom-made suit of white armor and bearing a flag with the words "Jesu et Maria" on it, Joan led the French army to victory, first taking Orleans, and then several others cities in the area. Finally, on the morning of July 17, 1429, in the city of Reims, Charles VII was crowned King of France with Joan and her flag beside him.

Things went downhill after that. With peacetime, Joan's army days were over and she was uncomfortable being forced to hang around court as part of the royal entourage. Many in the court were jealous and suspicious that an uneducated country girl had found such high favor with the King.

But once again war broke out with the English, and Joan was happy to get back in her armor to serve God and France. She was wounded and captured in a battle, and spent six months as the prisoner of the Duke of Burgundy. No effort was made by Charles or his court to aid her, and she was transferred over to the English who were ready and willing to destroy the French girl who had embarrassed them all with her military skill. After 4 months of endless hearings by a group of unscrupulous English judges and bishops, she was condemned to death as a witch and heretic. She was only 19 years old.

Twenty years later Pope Callistus III re-examined her case and completely vindicated her as an innocent maid who was falsely accused on trumped-up charges, and who should be considered a saint and martyr.

Today most of us would seek professional help if we started hearing voices urging us to start a war. But sometimes that small voice inside can inspire us to right a wrong, even if that means fighting against some pretty big odds. Joan tried to ignore her voices at first, arguing that it was impossible for a girl to lead an army, especially since she didn't know how to fight or even ride a horse. But she finally accepted the job with firm faith that God would be there beside her.

When you feel that you can't make a difference in your world because the odds are just too great, remember St. Joan. You can find the courage to win the daily battles if you keep in mind that God is always there with His love and support. All it takes is a little faith, a little hope, and maybe a good right hook from a heavenly martial arts instructor like Joan of Arc.

KEVIN
JUNE 3

Kevin was born of a noble family and was educated in a monastery run by his uncle. When the time came to build a second monastery, Kevin was chosen to be the Abbot, even though he was one of the youngest monks. When he heard that he had been selected for this high office, Kevin was shamed and afraid, because he felt there were older and wiser men who should have been chosen over him. So he ran away to become a hermit.

Kevin ended up by the Lake of Glendalough in Ireland. He lived in a hollow tree and ate nuts and berries for food, becoming a vegetarian out of his love for animals. Later he moved to a wooden hut. Soon other monks begged Kevin to be their spiritual leader. This time he agreed to be an abbot, and built the first of several monasteries at Glendalough that became an important center for learning as well as a major pilgrimage site.

Kevin got a reputation among the local peasants as a great veterinarian. Farmers started bringing sick animals to Kevin, and it seemed that any animal he touched was miraculously cured. Soon everyone in the area, including the local king, considered Kevin to be a saint.

So many legends are told about his great love of nature that he is often known as the Irish St. Francis of Assisi. It was said that St. Kevin gave sanctuary in his monastery to wild boars who were being pursued by the King's huntsmen, and even the hunting dogs showed him respect. Another legend tells how he fed his early followers with salmon caught for them on a regular basis by a friendly otter. But the all-time winner has to be the story of "St. Kevin and the Blackbird." When a particular blackbird laid its egg in Kevin's outstretched hand one day while he was preaching outdoors, the good abbot had such patience and gentleness that he remained with his hand outstretched until the egg hatched.

Kevin wasn't considered a saint just because he was great with animals. The people loved him because even though he spent a lot of time in prayer and meditation, he always had time to serve the needs of the common people outside the monastery walls.

A major debate in the history of the Church has been which is more important: the active life of service versus the contemplative life of prayer. St. Kevin came to the conclusion that we need both. Prayer and meditation is just as necessary as service to others in your community.

So be sure you make time in your busy schedule for volunteering as well as some time for quiet prayer. And here's a tip: if a friendly sea otter should start arriving with seafood, you'll definitely know you're on the right spiritual path.

BARNABAS
JUNE 11

We first hear about Barnabas in Chapter 4 of the Acts of the Apostles. St. Luke says he was a good man who sold his estates and gave all the proceeds to the apostles to be used for the common good. His name was originally Joseph, but the Apostles re-named him Barnabas which means "son of exhortation."

I originally thought Barnabas was the patron saint of second-bananas, that he was just one of the several young assistants that traveled with St. Paul and helped out with his missionary work. But when I actually went back to re-read the Acts, I realized I was completely wrong. Barnabas was the one who first introduced Paul to the rest of the apostles in Jerusalem and vouched for his conversion and good works. It seems Peter and the others were afraid that Paul was still out to persecute the Christians and that his conversion was just a trick. It was Barnabas who convinced them that Paul was a changed man, and that the change came about by his belief in Christ. A short time later, St. Peter sent Barnabas to take care of the Church at Antioch. After making a quick pastoral visit, Barnabas realized he could use some help, so he asked Paul to join him as a partner in spreading the Good News of Christ. So you might say that Barnabas gave Paul his first official job with the Church, with Barnabas as his mentor.

They were a great success among the Gentiles, and may have worked together in a "good cop/bad cop" kind of relationship. Paul was the great orator, full of fire and brimstone, and Barnabas appears to have been the behind-the-scenes wise man of few words. It fact when the two traveled to Greece, the people in one town were so amazed by their teachings and power to cure the sick that they were all convinced that Paul and Barnabas were Greek gods come down to earth: The Bible says that Barnabas was considered to be Jupiter/Zeus, the head of the gods, and it was Paul who was considered to be the lesser god Mercury/Hermes, because he was obviously the spokesman of Jupiter.

People held Barnabas in high regard, and he was evidently greatly respected by the Apostles back in Jerusalem. So why do we know more about St. Paul? Well, it looks like Paul had much better public relations skills. He was the one constantly making speeches, writing letters and getting into trouble with the authorities. Barnabas was just a good, low-keyed kind of pastor to his flock. Both were saints and both were responsible for the spread of Christianity to the Gentiles, but each had different talents and abilities. Eventually the two went their separate ways. Paul continued his missionary work with other partners like Silas and Timothy, while Barnabas settled down to take charge of the Christian community in Cyprus as a bishop.

What's the moral of this story? It's that we all have different talents and gifts. We don't have to be rich and famous to make a difference in someone's life; we can use whatever we have in the service of Christ. You might even be able to help someone else become a saint. Even if we never get our 15 minutes of fame on the 6 o'clock news, we can still be superstars in the eyes of God. Just ask St. Barnabas.

ANTHONY OF PADUA
JUNE 13

When many people lose something (especially those who went to parochial school), the first thing they do is pray to St. Anthony. All around the world, people implore his intercession to find everything from lost keys to lost souls. How he got this reputation is a long story.

Born in 1195 to a noble Portuguese family from Lisbon, young Ferdinand decided on a life of devotion early on. He first joined the local Augustinian seminary, but later entered the Franciscan order. Anthony was the name he took when he became a Franciscan friar in 1221.

After ordination, he was sent to Morocco with the intention of preaching the Gospel there. Illness struck him down almost as soon as he arrived and he had to turn back. More bad luck prevailed when his ship was driven off-course to Sicily. A long trudge up the foot of Italy followed, until he came to Assisi to attend the Franciscan General Convention of 1221. Here he met the great St. Francis, and was appointed to the lonely hermitage of San Paolo. Basically, he was sent on retreat to discover what God planned as his mission in life. It wasn't long before his superiors realized that his real talents were in preaching rather than contemplative prayer, and before long he was on the road again, this time to Lombardy in northern Italy. Besides preaching, he was appointed as the first theology lecturer to the friars. Until this time, St. Francis had felt that books and higher education were not in keeping with Gospel simplicity. St. Anthony convinced him that possessing the knowledge of Scripture as well as other books of theology could bring the brothers closer to knowledge of God and help them impart that knowledge to the people they served. St. Francis was convinced, St. Anthony got the job, and the friars got permission to own books and get an education.

Contemporary records tell us that St. Anthony was not the tall, ascetic-looking saint that we always see in statues and paintings. Inquiring medieval minds tell us he was short and a little overweight, but he attracted people to him, so much so that the churches were not big enough to hold all those who wanted to listen. He was forced to go out to the marketplace to deliver his sermons. Many were converted after hearing his words, delivered in a strong and powerful voice.

High offices were offered to him, but he preferred to take his message directly to the common people, so instead of opting for a choice assignment in Rome, Anthony settled in the small town of Padua, and remained there until his death in 1231. He was canonized just one year later.

Which brings us back to St. Anthony of Padua as the patron saint of lost articles. How a Franciscan became the manager of a celestial lost-and-found department is uncertain. One legend says that when a brother friar stole his psalmbook, St. Anthony prayed it would be returned. The guilty friar was overcome with remorse and brought the book back.

Even though we usually implore St. Anthony for help us finding things, maybe we could also ask him for the opposite. He just might be glad to hear a request to lose something for once: things like a bad attitude, or lack of self-discipline, or a lack of patience with others. And, yeah, the loss of a few pounds couldn't hurt either.

Peter
June 29

From the Gospels we know he was a Galilean and that his original home was in Bethsaida. Peter is the patron saint of fisherman, and he was also the first apostle called by Christ. This happened while he was casting his nets into the Sea of Galilee with Andrew, his brother and partner in the family fishing business. His name was actually "Simon" at the time. Jesus renamed him "Peter," which means "rock" in Aramaic.

He was not an educated man, but then ordinary working people rarely were in those days. We know he was a married man, because the New Testament mentions Christ going to his home and healing Peter's mother-in-law. Contrary to most television sit-coms, she appears to have been a very nice mother-in-law, because as soon as she was cured, she jumped right up and cooked a great dinner for Jesus, Peter, and the rest of his friends.

It's also obvious from reading the New Testament that Peter was considered the lead and spokesman for all the Apostles when he said such profound things as, "Thou art the Christ, the Son of the living God." After the Ascension of Christ, Peter still had the leading role. It was Peter who was responsible for the conversion of Cornelius the centurion, deciding the issue that the old practices of Jewish law, such as food rituals and not associating with Gentiles, should give way to the new practices of Christianity.

But it's also obvious that he was a man with a lot of faults who made more than his share of mistakes. Peter was the guy who never did things halfway. He would jump out of a boat and try to walk on the water, all the while declaring his undying love for Christ. He also lost his confidence and denied Jesus not once, but three times.

He may have been bull-headed some times and unsure the rest, but he was always passionate when it came to his beliefs about Christ and about spreading the Gospel. He ended up a martyr for the faith in Rome during the reign of the Emperor Nero.

Peter made some major mistakes and did some selfish things, but he repented, was forgiven, and learned to love and forgive others. He also gives us a great example to follow as we struggle to become disciples of Christ. We all need to learn how to forgive others, forgive ourselves, and then begin again. If it worked for a tough guy like St. Peter, it will work for all of us, too.

ELIZABETH OF PORTUGAL
JULY 4

She was born the daughter of King Peter III of Aragon in 1271. Her great aunt was St. Elizabeth of Hungary, and she is better known in Spain and Portugal as "Saint Isabella."

Elizabeth was married at age 12 to King Denis of Portugal, who appears to have been a pretty rotten husband. He neglected her and was unfaithful, so she devoted her days to helping her subjects while she raised their two children, Alonzo and Constance. Queen Elizabeth had a regular schedule for morning and evening prayer. She provided food and lodging for the poor and for people traveling on pilgrimages. She even built a hospital and orphanage, and helped found and finance a convent of Franciscan nuns (also known as the "Poor Clares").

She was also an excellent political ambassador, and her qualities as a peacemaker were notable. She averted a war between Ferdinand IV of Castile and her brother, James II of Aragon.

King Denis became seriously ill in 1324, and Elizabeth became his personal nurse, never leaving his room except to go to church. During his long illness the king repented of his immoral life and begged her forgiveness for all the rotten things he had done. After he died the following year, she joined the Franciscan Third Order and lived the rest of her life in a little house she built near the Poor Clare convent she had founded years before.

She had considered becoming a nun, but decided against it in order to keep the king's inheritance and be free to give to charitable causes as she saw fit. Nuns took a vow of poverty, which meant Elizabeth would have to give up all her money and property and turn it over to her son. She knew

Alonzo would waste it all on wild parties instead of using it to help his subjects, so she decided to keep control of the funds by becoming a Franciscan lay-sister instead. Third Order members take a vow of simplicity instead of absolute poverty.

St. Elizabeth loved her son; she just wasn't blind to his faults. And she proves it's possible to be a good person, live a simple life, and be financially astute, all at the same time. Her story shows us that you can successfully combine tough love with a kind heart to make your little corner of the world a better place for all.

CAMILLUS
JULY 14

He was born in Italy in 1550. By the time he was a teenager he was already 6 feet, 6 inches tall, and at age 17 he went off with his father to fight with the Venetians against the Turks. He soon contracted a painful leg disease that afflicted him for the rest of his life.

In 1571 Camillus was admitted to the San Giacomo Hospital for Incurables in Rome, but was thrown out 9 months later due to his bad temper and constant complaining. He went back to active service in the war against the Turks. He became addicted to gambling and alcohol during his second tour of duty. After he was mustered out in 1574, he quickly gambled away his savings, his armor, and everything he owned including the shirt off his back. It wasn't until he was down and out in Naples that he finally saw the error of his ways and vowed to straighten up.

He found work as a day-laborer helping to build the new Franciscan church in town. When the church was finished 2 years later he asked to join the Franciscan Order. They wouldn't take him because of his bad leg (it seems he had some kind of disgusting sores on his leg that never did heal). So he went back to the San Giacomo Hospital, not as a patient this time but as a nurse, and devoted all his time to the sick. People took notice of his great ability and charity, and he was soon promoted up the ranks to hospital superintendent.

To make himself better able to serve the sick spiritually as well as physically, he studied for the priesthood and was ordained. He founded a religious order called "The Ministers of the Sick." Members were all men trained in nursing techniques by Camillus himself. They lived together in a house with set times for communal prayer, and were bound to serve those infected with the plague, sick prisoners, and those dying in hospices: basically all the patients nobody wanted.

Camillus and his nursing brothers pioneered many modern medical practices, such as the importance of fresh air, the need to isolate infectious patients, and the use of special diets. Members of his Order served with the troops fighting in Hungary and Croatia in 1595-1601, making them the first recorded military nursing units.

He had to found a second community in Naples to keep up with all his new volunteers, and then several others. With his growing fame as a healer and his medical services to the military, many members of the Italian nobility donated money and property to St. Camillus. By the time of his death at age 64, he had received enough funds to built 8 hospitals. So it's not surprising to learn that he shares the honor of patron saint of nurses along with St. Elizabeth of Hungary.

If you're in the situation of being forced to make a career change and are afraid of the unknown, don't worry. It just might be God's way of preparing you for better things. Just remember our friend, Camillus: soldier, nurse, hospital administrator, religious leader...and saint.

Bonaventure
July 15

He was born Giovanni di Fidanza in the village of Bagnore near Rome in 1221. Legend has it he got the name "Bonaventure" when he was 4 years old and seriously ill. His parents took him to see St. Francis of Assisi in hope that the saint could cure him. St. Francis cured the boy and said, "O! Buona ventura!" (Oh, what good fortune!).

He entered the Franciscan Order in 1238, and was later elected Minister General of the Order. He did much to reform and mediate internal problems between rival factions among the Franciscans. These were the days of huge arguments about how strict the rule should be, if education should be allowed, if money was evil, and whether or not the friars should accept high
offices in the Church.

Bonaventure was an outstanding scholar and eventually took a degree in theology at the Sorbonne in Paris the same time as his good friend and classmate, the Dominican scholar, St. Thomas Aquinas. He gained the title of "Seraphic Doctor" and was considered a great philosopher, theologian and author of many books and essays on religion.

In 1265 he refused the position of Archbishop of York. Officially it was said that he didn't feel worthy of high office and begged to be excused. But it also may have been due to the fact that he would have to move from Italy and deal with the cold, wet winters of England. We visited with friends near York last December and it was freezing! At any event the Pope excused him. But he did accept a promotion seven years later when he was asked to become cardinal and bishop of Albano in Italy. The story goes that when the papal delegation arrived with his official papers and cardinal's red hat, St. Bonaventure was in the friary kitchen, washing dishes, since it was his turn for kitchen duty. He made the astonished delegation wait until he was finished.

There's a good lesson here for the rest of us. We can't all do great things, but we can all do small things in a great way. All of us have different talents and abilities, but one talent is not better than another or less valuable in the scheme of things. St. Bonaventure was a famous theologian and author, but he didn't consider his community kitchen duties beneath his other skills. It was all done for love of God and his fellow friars. Whatever God puts in our path, we have the chance to decide to make it a great act of love. St. Bonaventure would say that was the right path to take. Especially if that path leads to warm winters in sunny Italy.

MARY MAGDALENE
JULY 22

Have you ever been falsely accused and mislabeled by mistake because of where you come from or whom you associate with? Poor Mary has had a bad rap for centuries that's really a complete misunderstanding. She has unfortunately been identified with the "sinful woman" who anointed Jesus' feet at house of Simon the Pharisee. And since this woman is often thought to have been a prostitute, Mary Magdalene gets stuck with that label as well.

But if you read the Scriptures, our Mary is only described as someone who had 7 devils cast out of her by Jesus. So she might have been mentally ill or subject to seizures, but there is nothing in the New Testament to indicate she was any kind of notorious wanton woman. People may mistakenly think of her as a woman with a shady past, but the Bible actually is full of wonderful, loving things written about her. And to tell you the truth, Mary Magdalene comes off as a much better and braver follower of Jesus than all of the apostles. In His darkest hour on the cross, she was there. On Easter Sunday when the women came to properly prepare Christ's body for burial, she was one of them. And Mary Magdalene was the first person to see, be greeted by, and finally recognize the Risen Christ in the garden by the empty tomb.

Legend has it that she, along with Lazarus and his sisters Martha and Mary, became missionaries to France.

Mary was probably in the audience when Jesus gave the Sermon on the Mount and said, "Blessed are you when you suffer insults and persecution of every kind for My sake." We tend to think that only applies to the bad old days when they arrested Christians and threw them to the lions. But in more subtle ways, it still applies today.

Maybe you thought about going to church more often, but your friends teased you about it, so you stopped going altogether. Or maybe you've been struggling to give up some bad habits, but those around you say, "Why bother? You'll never change."

The people back in Mary Magdalene's hometown may have ridiculed her as a crazy person who was just no good. But Christ never did. He saw into her heart and soul and healed her. Her life changed, and it didn't matter what anyone else could say or do. What mattered was that she was a follower of Christ, and that she was loved.

So when the going gets rough and the world is getting you down, remember the example of St. Mary: trust God; see all nor be afraid; and always know that you are greatly loved.

JOHN VIANNEY
AUGUST 4

He was born near Lyons, France in 1786, three years before the French Revolution. He spent his days taking care of the sheep and cattle on his father's farm on the outskirts of town. When he was 18 he decided he wanted to become a priest, so he asked his father's permission. But his dad needed his help on the farm, so he wasn't allowed to leave for the seminary until 2 years later.

John was one of the world's worst students. He had no natural aptitude for reading, writing, science or math. But he struggled and persevered. He barely managed to pass the first level, but was not accepted to the college-level seminary because he couldn't remember enough Latin. One of the theology professors recognized something special in John and gave him private tutoring. After 3 years of intensive study, John was considered just competent enough to be ordained a priest in 1815, and was assigned as the curate-assistant to his priest mentor and friend, because no other parish would take him.

Father John took his new vocation very seriously. First, he personally visited every family in his parish, and started catechism classes for the children. Then he decided to inspire the people to love Christ and one another through sermons and lectures, both on Sundays and in the confessional. His counseling work in the confessional was what brought the little, obscure curate national attention.

Those were the days before anyone had ever heard of psychologists, marriage counselors, or family therapists. If you had problems, you either worked them alone, or else you confided in your local parish priest. If you were lucky enough, you might get some good advice and support, but more likely you would only be told to say more "Our Fathers" and "Hail Marys," and offer up your sorrows to God.

John was one of the great self-taught counselors and therapists of all time. People from all around the French countryside came to talk with him in the little village of Ars. He ended up spending 11 hours a day in the confessional in winter, and up to 16 hours a day in the summer. His little church became a major pilgrimage stop: everybody who was anybody had to come and get advice from the Curé de Ars. It was recorded that in the last two years before he died, 100,000 people had made the pilgrimage to Ars, France.

So how did the world's worst student become such a wise counselor? What was Father John's secret? He always said that God gave him the gift of simply being the world's best listener. He would listen to people who came to him for help, and then with a few questions, help them find the answer in their hearts.

St. John's advice is just as relevant today. Instead of always having to get the last word, just sit back and truly listen to your family, your friends, and to everyone else who just needs someone to talk to. And while we're at it, maybe it's a good idea to be quiet and just listen when we have a problem ourselves. For only then will we be able to hear God's small, still answer in our hearts.

DOMINIC
AUGUST 8

Dominic was born in Castile, Spain in 1170. He entered the priesthood, and eventually became the head of the canons (the clergy who were the staff of the cathedral and conducted the daily worship services) in the city of Osma. He was chosen in 1206 to accompany his bishop on a visit to southern France, to an area held by the Albigenses. They were a heretical sect who believed in two Gods: the God of light, goodness, truth and spirit; and another God of evil and darkness. The idea was that the evil God created the world and the flesh, and the good God created the souls of men, so that life was a constant struggle between the evil flesh and the good spirit. Dominic and the bishop undertook the study of the Albigensian beliefs and engaged in public debates with their opponents. In fact Dominic was so successful that in 1206 he founded a convent for a group of 9 nuns, all of whom were Albigenses converts.

Dominic continued to preach and debate wherever he could, and then considered the idea of starting a religious order for men. He was convinced that one of the major obstacles to the conversion of heretics was the wealth and worldliness of the clergy, so he was determined that his order of friars would accept simplicity and poverty like the Franciscans. Dominic's idea was that his Order of Preachers would not be like monks who were strict contemplatives locked up in a monastery, but friars who would unite a contemplative prayer life with preaching and teaching. They were to devote themselves to the study of philosophy and theology in order to combat false doctrine by logical and educated argument, rather than by force. He opened his first friary in 1216 in Toulouse, France with an international cast: eight Frenchmen, seven Spaniards, and one Englishman.

Dominic became well-known through Europe, and was invited by Pope Honorius IV to come to Rome and lecture on theology. His eloquence as a speaker made the whole city take notice and increased his fame and that of the Dominican Order. His friars become the leading professors at the Universities of Paris and Bologna.

Dominic set up other friaries in France, Spain and Italy, but spent most of his time as a theology professor at the University of Bologna until his death in 1221. But he lived to see his Order spread as far as Poland, Scandinavia, Palestine, and England.

Dominic felt that we can never solve our differences by ranting and raving about sin and degradation. He teaches us that the Christian way is to use kindness, and to give a good example by leading a life of faith, hope, and charity. We don't have to win every argument by destroying the opposition. Take a lesson from St. Dominic: it's always better to have love than to have the last word.

CLARE OF ASSISI
AUGUST 11

Clare was born in 1194, the daughter of a very wealthy family in Assisi. When she was 18, she heard a sermon by St. Francis. She was so moved by it that she decided to follow his example and vow herself to a life of poverty as a nun. Her family was horrified and tried to keep her locked up at home, but one night she slipped out by the servant's entrance and went to see St. Francis and his friars. He accepted her into the Franciscan Order and got her placed in a nearby Benedictine convent. Later a house was found for her, attached to the Church of San Damiano, and she was soon joined by two of her sisters.

Clare wrote down a rule of life for her nuns that was far stricter than even St. Francis' rule for men. And it was a pretty austere lifestyle for formerly wealthy women who had been accustomed to fine food and servants. They weren't allowed to wear shoes or sandals, they slept on the floor, never ate meat, and kept silence as much as possible. But the three sisters felt immensely happy and free.

When Clare's father died, her mother gave away the money in her daughters' dowries and joined them in the convent. When the Order of Poor Clares was officially formed, St. Francis suggested Clare for their superior, but Clare refused the position until she turned 21. They devoted themselves to prayer, nursing the sick, and taking care of the poor and neglected. The sisters of her order are still known as the Poor Clares.

Within a few years Clare sent other nuns to found several other convents in Italy, France and Germany. Clare was abbess of her convent in Assisi for over 40 years. She herself never left Assisi, handling all the business for her Order via letters to her other convents across Europe. Two different popes, not to mention assorted cardinals and bishops, came to see her for advice on spiritual issues.

Clare is also considered the patron saint of television. One Christmas Day she was so ill she could not attend Mass with her nuns. While lying alone in bed, she saw a vision of the infant Jesus on the wall opposite her bed. At the same time she could hear the service being celebrated at the Church of St. Francis a mile away, including all the singing and music....not unlike big-screen T.V. with stereophonic sound.

Clare and Francis remained best friends for the rest of their lives, even though they only saw each other face-to-face a few times after Clare became a cloistered nun. Although their meetings were mostly by letter, their love for one another as brother and sister on the journey together to follow Christ was a constant source of happiness and family support in both their lives.

Having a family to support us in our life of faith is a great gift. Being part of an extended family that we worship with on Sundays can be a source of comfort, love, and affirmation. St. Clare used her wisdom and sense of peace and calm to help her immediate family, her convent sisters, and even her brother-saint Francis become closer to Christ. May her example inspire us to go forth and do likewise among our own extended families today.

FIACRE
SEPTEMBER 1

Fiacre was a 7th century Irish hermit who started off hating people. His motto was, "I want to be alone." He felt Ireland was getting too crowded, so he left to find greater solitude in France. St. Faro, who was the local bishop, gave him land for a hermitage, and Fiacre decided to plant a large herb, flower and vegetable garden. His skill with plants got him the job as the patron saint of gardeners, and he's usually depicted in paintings holding a shovel, watering can, or some other gardening tool. Fiacre also built a small chapel, and figured he would happily spend the rest of his life in prayer and solitude.

Then Bishop Faro starting asking the hermit for advice on the use of medicinal plants when illness struck the area. It wasn't long before the local people starting talking about the hermit herbalist who prescribed medicines that sometimes miraculously cured the sick. Soon Fiacre found himself unhappily surrounded by lots of visitors. Then it happened: out of the blue he realized that while he was looking for solitude, God had something else in mind. The former hermit expanded the garden and built a small hospice so that he could care for the sick who came to seek his medical advice.

Soon a village grew up around his house and famous garden, with a monastery, convent, expanded hospital, inns, shops, and shrines. It became known as Saint-Fiacre-in-Seine-et-Marne, and was a popular tourist stop on the pilgrimage circuit, something like a religious health spa.

An interesting side note is that St. Fiacre is also considered the patron saint of taxi-drivers. It seems that back in the late 1600s, the first horse-drawn hackney cabs for hire used to wait in front of the grand Hotel Saint-Fiacre in Paris. The cabs got to be known as "fiacres," and St. Fiacre got promoted to another heavenly assignment by simply having the right hotel named after him at the right time.

Sometimes our true vocation in life drops right in our laps while we're busy making other plans. Fiacre was convinced that his life was perfect as a hermit, and he wanted to have nothing to do with his fellow man. He was absolutely convinced all his time should be spent alone in prayer. Fortunately for all those sick people, he changed his mind.

St. Fiacre's green thumb not only brought beauty to his garden, but also life-saving medicine to relieve the pain and suffering of the people he originally had tried so hard to avoid. He finally saw God's plan, and changed the focus of his life to serve others rather than himself. St. Fiacre shows us that we're actually reaching out to God when we reach out to help one another. Finding solitude in your secret garden is still a wonderful thing; just don't forget to go out and share the roses with those who need your love.

HILDEGARD OF BINGEN
SEPTEMBER 17

Hildegard was born in Germany in 1098. She became a Benedictine nun at age 15 and lived an uneventful life for the next 17 years. At age 42 she was elected prioress of her convent. Then things started happening.

She started having dreams and visions during her meditation sessions in church. The Pope heard about her visions and set up a commission to investigate them. Hildegard passed with flying colors. She wrote descriptions of her visions in several books at the urging of the pope. Actually, she dictated them to a monk secretary, Brother Volmar, since Hildegard never learned to write proper Latin (all theological books, indeed, all textbooks of the time in any subject had to be done in Latin, the language of scholars). Her father-confessor, who was the local Benedictine abbot, assigned Volmar as her full-time secretary and scribe for the next ten years, and her books were all completed in this partnership. She may not have been great at spelling and grammar, but she was a rather good artist, and she personally illustrated some of the books. They were allegorical stories along the lines of Dante's ***Divine Comedy***, and became very popular religious reading in Europe at the time.

She was a true Renaissance woman. Besides handling all the business affairs for her large and growing convent, she was an artist, architect, musician, song-writer, playwright, and herbalist. Her music and Georgian chant hymns have become very popular the last few years. It's good to see that 900 years later, Sister Hildegard's books, music, art, holistic medicine, mysticism and theology ideas are as popular today as they were was when she was considered the "Dear Abby" of the 12th century. She never hesitated to stand up and say or do what needed to be done, simply because she was woman. When a pope or emperor needed a verbal whack on the head, she wasn't afraid to give them their medicine, just like St. Catherine of Sienna 200 years later.

Following the way of Christ doesn't mean you put away your talents and give up your special gifts to simply pray and meditate in solitude. We all need to share those special gifts and talents that are uniquely ours to bring peace and love and happiness to others. St. Hildegard would say that's the only way to have true peace and happiness in our own lives. And that kind of spiritual wisdom from a Renaissance Wonderwoman is pretty good advice for all of us today.

MATTHEW
SEPTEMBER 21

The patron saint of bookkeepers, accountants, and customs officials, Matthew started off in life as a tax collector, a job about as popular in Jesus' time as IRS auditors are today. Matthew himself states in his Gospel that tax collectors and sinners were considered one and the same. Even worse was the fact that he worked for the Romans, getting a percentage of all the money he collected. So as well as being considered a sinner and holding an unsavory job, he was also considered something of a traitor to his own people. And yet Christ personally chose this controversial guy to be one of his apostles.

Matthew was just another despised tax collector until he met Jesus and his life changed forever. Jesus said, "Follow me," and Matthew left his job, his wealth, and his friends to follow this unknown young rabbi from Nazareth. Now the significant part of this story is that Christ, as a devout Jew, should never even have *spoken* to Matthew, much less make him a friend and apostle. Christ didn't see the job, or social position, or other people's opinions. He looked into Matthew's heart and saw the true man who would become a great missionary and eventually be martyred for the faith in Ethiopia.

How often today are we more likely to be impressed by someone who has a job as a doctor or lawyer or business executive rather than someone who is a grocery checker or gardener or garbage collector...or even, God forbid...someone who works for the Internal Revenue Service? Fortunately, God judges us not on the color of our money but on the content of our character.

St. Matthew was personally touched by God and went on to write the first of the four Gospels that have been read by millions of people throughout the centuries. Proof positive that God has plans for all of us – no matter how taxing our present occupation and no matter how many past penalties we've incurred for late or incomplete returns.

FRANCIS OF ASSISI
OCTOBER 4

Francis was born John Bernadone, the son of a wealthy cloth merchant. His parents called him "Francis," because his mother was from France, and his father had been involved in a lucrative business deal in Paris at the time of his birth in 1181.

He lived the life of a typical medieval rich kid: fine clothes, lots of money, always looking for a good time with his friends. He was even something of a medieval rock and roll star in Assisi. When he was a teenager, he decided to become a troubadour or wandering minstrel. His mother bought him a lute and music lessons and a fancy costume so that Francis could entertain at parties around town.

Then a war of sorts broke out between Assisi and the nearby town of Perugia. The nobles in Assisi asked for volunteers to fight the Perugians, and Francis and his friends all signed up. Their families bought them all suits of armor and fine horses, and Francis was thrilled with the chance of achieving fame and glory as a knight. The best and brightest of Assisi rode off to the sounds of trumpets and cheers from the townspeople. But the glory was short lived.

They soon discovered that even a minor war was an ugly business that could bring injury and death. Francis and some of the rest were captured and spent several months as prisoners of war before they were finally released. When he came home to Assisi, he was broken in spirit and in health. He spend his time in prayer and meditation to find out what God had in store for him, since all his plans had gone by the wayside. While praying in the dilapidated church of San Damiano outside Assisi, Francis heard the Crucifix over the altar speak to him and say, "Francis, repair my church which you see is falling down." Francis was overjoyed and took the commission literally, rebuilding the church stone by stone and living a simple life as a hermit-pilgrim. Eventually other friends joined him, and soon he was the leader of a religious order of friars (and later a Second Order of nuns and a Third Order for lay people), that changed medieval Italy, and eventually, the whole world.

When he decided to change his life, he did it dramatically. Instead of the expensive clothes of his youth, Francis wore a simple brown pilgrim's robe and went barefoot; he kept giving away his sandals to someone more in need. He found an overwhelming joy in seeing God in all creation: the sun, moon, plants, animals...all the world and everything in it.

St. Francis was the one who invented the custom of setting up a miniature Nativity scene at Christmas. One December he was staying in the town of Greccio. He suddenly got the idea of showing the townspeople the wonder of the Christ Child lying in a feed trough in a common stable. He set up small statues of Mary and Joseph, shepherds and Bethlehem townspeople in the local church, and brought in a real donkey, an ox, and a few lambs and sheep. And there in the manger he placed a little Baby Jesus for all the people to see when they arrived for Midnight Mass on Christmas Eve. The nativity crèche became an annual Christmas event and a wonderful custom that continues to this day.

The message of St. Francis for us today is not so much poverty as simplicity. The rich young man from Assisi came to realize that simple joys and simple wonders can bring us closer to the love of God and one another. It's a lesson in love that's just as relevant today.

FRANCIS BORGIA
OCTOBER 10

Francis was born Francisco de Borja y Aragon in 1510, and was the great-grandson of a Pope (Alexander VI), a King (Ferdinand V of Aragon), and the cousin of an Emperor (Charles V).

He was married at age 19 and was made a marquis. Ten years later his cousin, the Emperor, made him Viceroy of Barcelona. When his father died, Francis also became the Duke of Gandia. In spite of his multiple leadership jobs, he devoted as much time as possible to prayer and mediation, much to the ridicule of his friends and relatives at court.

His wife Eleanor died in 1546, leaving him with 8 children, the youngest only 8 years old. He asked his good friend, St. Ignatius of Loyola (founder of the Jesuit Order), about giving up his privileged life at court and becoming a priest. Ignatius gave him the wise advice of staying home and making sure his children were all established and provided for. In the meantime, he suggested Francis study theology at the Jesuit University of Gandia.

After 3 years of study he received a doctorate in theology. He then received permission from the Emperor to transfer all his titles and estates to his eldest son, Charles, and was ordained a priest in 1551. The "Duke turned Jesuit" was a big celebrity at the time, and when Francis celebrated his first public Mass, the crowds (including all his children and even a few grandchildren) were so big that they had to set up the altar on the steps outside so that everyone could participate.

Becoming a priest was also good for his health and fitness program. As a duke, all that rich food and fine wine made Francis a very fat man. In fact it was a joke at court that his belt was so big it could go around three normally-sized guys. His time spent in study for the priesthood coincided with his choosing a simple lifestyle and diet, so by the end of 3 years he had become a lean, mean, preaching machine, and stayed that way for the rest of his life.

Due to his management abilities and royal connections, St. Ignatius made him Commissary-General of the Jesuits in Spain and Portugal, and Francis established several colleges in those countries. He was no friend to the Spanish Inquisition and publicly condemned their abuses. Because of the Inquisition's power in the Spanish court, Francis was forced to leave his own country, and ended up getting transferred back to headquarters in Rome. His fight with the Inquisition won him the admiration of the common people as well as many church leaders in Italy. He was elected Father General of the Society of Jesus, which made him the Head Jesuit throughout the world.

The Pope sent him on an embassy tour to Spain, Portugal and France a few years later, and crowds came out everywhere to see him and hear him preach. He also managed to keep in touch with all his many children and grandchildren throughout his travels around Europe.

The poor and the ignorant were always his special concern. He treated everyone he met with courtesy and charm. He had a passion to guide, counsel and console all in need of help. In other words, he was the perfect Dad. He was a father to his 8 children, a father to his fellow-Jesuits, and a good father to his various church congregations.

So even though it's way past June, let's all wish "Happy Father's Day" to St. Francis this October 10th.. God knows, the man's a saint who has definitely earned it.

JOHN OF CAPISTRANO
OCTOBER 23

Inquiring medieval minds might find it interesting to note that there is a group of saints from the Middle Ages who turned their lives around and decided to serve God only after serving time in prison. Technically they were all prisoners of war rather than hard-boiled criminals. St. Francis of Assisi, St. John of Capistrano, and St. Ignatius Loyola, to name a few, used their time in prison as what you might call a forced monastic retreat. Of course it helped that monasteries at that time were a lot like prisons: bare cells, bad food, and no girlfriends.

John was born in the village of Capistrano in central Italy in 1385. His father was a German Baron, and his mother was Italian nobility. He studied law, got married, and was named governor of Perugia by the King of Naples. He was sent to mediate peace terms in a war between two warring factions, but ended up in prison as a hostage.

Prison gave him the time to examine his life. By the time he got out, he had decided to join the Franciscans (it seems his wife died rather young). Legend has it that after his release, St. John came back to Perugia riding backwards on a donkey, wearing a big paper hat on which he had written all the sins of his past life (this is starting to sound a lot like "Yankee Doodle"). People laughed and kids threw all sorts of garbage at him, but he somehow managed to steer his donkey to the doorstep of the local Franciscan friary. After having made such an impressive entrance, he asked to be admitted as a novice. The superiors must have considered him to be sincere, because he was eventually ordained a priest in 1420.

His previous talents as a great administrator came to good use and he was responsible for handing reforms in the various Franciscan orders of the time. He received a lot of fame as a great preacher, and was sent by the Pope as a special emissary all over Europe to promote the Crusades.

The seventh of the California Missions was established in his name in 1776. And even though he's not such a well-known saint these days (more people know about the swallows that return every March 19th to Mission San Juan Capistrano than anything about him), St. John is a good example of the good you can do even if you're forced to change careers. A former lawyer and ex-governor becomes a great church administrator and lecturer in the service of God. Proving once again that God has special goals for each of us, no matter how different our own best-laid plans may be. All we have to do is find the time to pray and listen to that small, still voice that says, "Follow Me."

MARTIN DE PORRES
NOVEMBER 3

Martin was born in Lima, Peru in 1579. His father was a Spanish knight and his mother was a black freewoman from Panama. Martin was dark-skinned like his mother and older sister, which bothered his prejudiced father no end. Dad soon left Martin and his sister with their mother, and while it appears he did pay child support, Don Juan de Porres never bothered to see his children again.

Their mother managed to make up for their missing father by showering them with great love and affection. When he was 12, his mother managed to get Martin apprenticed as a barber-surgeon so that he could make a good living. Barbers in those days also functioned as dentists, as well as providing other medical services such as setting broken bones, and mixing herbs for medicines. Martin was very good at his job, and it was during this time that he decided to join the Third Order of St. Dominic. Three years later he became a professed lay-brother and went to live at the Dominican Priory in Lima.

Besides acting as the herbalist, barber, and gardener at the priory, Martin's biggest job was to handle the distribution of alms to the poor of the city. He was great at collecting money and goods from the businessmen in town for those in need. Martin was instrumental in establishing an orphanage and foundling hospital, and later took on the job of caring for the physical and spiritual needs of the slaves who were brought to Peru from Africa. He was also an animal lover, and established a home for abandoned cats and dogs at his sister's house.

He became a well-known member of the community due to the great love he showed to all: young and old, rich and poor, black and white, slave and free. Whether you needed a blanket, a shirt, a meal, a prayer, a home for your cat, some good advice, or just a smile and a kind word, St. Martin was the brother people stood in line for hours to visit.

He never had much formal education and was never ordained a priest, but he won the admiration of his religious community, so much so that he was elected the spiritual director of the priory, in charge of all the other priests and brothers. When he died in 1639, he was carried to his grave by cardinals, bishops, and noblemen who came from across the country to honor the black hero who later became the patron saint of social workers and barbers.

Why was he so loved and respected by people from all walks of life? Maybe it was because Martin felt called to serve everyone, regardless of religion, race, gender, or social standing. In his eyes, even dogs, cats, and mice were worthwhile creatures of God, and all part of one loving family.

So when you hear about racial and political problems across this country or across the world, don't give up hope. Like St. Martin, remember that you, too, can change the world, a little at a time, by a smile, a gift, and a prayer.

CHARLES BORROMEO
NOVEMBER 4

Charles was born into an early Renaissance lifestyle of the fabulously rich and powerful. His mother was a member of the powerful Medici family of Italy, and his uncle eventually became Pope Pius IV. At age 21, Charles was made a cardinal and Papal Secretary of State before he was even ordained a priest. In those days only bishops had to be ordained as holding a true clerical position. Cardinals were political appointments of the Pope, and, as such, could technically remain laymen. It was during this period of his life that he decided to join the Franciscan Third Order (the same one I belong to for both lay people and clergy who want to be part of the Franciscan Order but who don't have to live in a formal religious community like a monastery or convent).

After being a cardinal for two years, he was forced to make a decision. When his father died, he was given the chance to resign from religious life, get married, and become the head of his wealthy family, all with the Church's blessing. He amazed everyone by officially renouncing his right to the head-of-the-family job and deciding to become an ordained priest in order to serve others. Coincidentally, the day after his ordination, he was promoted to the rank of Archbishop of Milan.

Archbishop Charles helped his uncle, the pope, to put into action the reforms of the Council of Trent of 1562. He also showed great concern for the poor and sick of his diocese of Milan when they were stricken by a devastating plague in 1576. Charles quickly set up hospitals and soup kitchens, and personally visited the patients when many of the clergy left their posts to escape to healthier areas.

He died at the age of 46 and was canonized about 20 years later. The second of the California Missions (San Carlos) established by the Franciscan padres in 1771 was named after him.

Even though Charles held an influential position in the Church, he was well known throughout Italy for his humility and mission of service to others from all walks of life and all social classes. Another message here is that having money is <u>not</u> the root of all evil. The love of money that blinds you to other things and other persons is the problem. Using your talents, monetary and otherwise, for God's good purposes is what makes all the difference.

So the next time you're tempted to say "I gave at the office," remember St. Charles. He'd be the first to say, "The world is our office: time to clock in and get to work for the Lord."

MARGARET OF SCOTLAND
NOVEMBER 16

Here's a saint that all the married ladies will love. If it's true that opposites attract, then St. Margaret and her husband, King Malcolm III, must have been made for each other. Margaret was refined, cultured, and educated. Malcolm was rough, coarse, and uncouth...your typical medieval oaf. That is, until Margaret came along.

She was born of a noble family (they were related to St. Edward the Confessor, who was King of England in 1042). Her family sought political asylum with King Malcolm Canmore of Scotland to get away from William the Conqueror. They say Margaret was as beautiful as she was good and talented, and it wasn't long before Malcolm started taking notice. They were married in 1070 when she was 24, and apparently lived happily ever after.

Margaret was a great influence on Malcolm and accomplished the almost impossible task of actually changing her husband. She taught him manners and social graces, and even got him to go to church on Sundays. She also formed one of the first altar guilds among the ladies of the court. They did embroidery for vestments and altar furnishings for several churches that the king and queen founded throughout Scotland.

They had eight royal offspring who all turned out rather well. One daughter married Henry I of England and became known as Good Queen Maud, while their youngest son, David, also became a saint when he occupied the Scottish throne.

St. Margaret teaches us being a saint doesn't have to be a bleak life of suffering and penance. Through her prayers and good nature she managed to bring art, education, culture, and love not just to King Malcolm, but to all the people of Scotland.

So if you feel that the only way to sainthood is by suffering in silence, just remember St. Margaret of Scotland. She did it all with love, culture, and by keeping her husband in line.

ELIZABETH OF HUNGARY
NOVEMBER 19

It may seem like some saints could hardly wait until their respective spouses died so that they could enter monasteries and convents, found religious orders, and do other "saintly" things. But not Princess Elizabeth of Hungary. She loved being a wife and the mother of four children.

She was born in 1207, engaged at age 3, and married when she turned 14 to Prince Louis IV of Thuringia. It was a very happy marriage, and she stayed madly in love with her husband until he died fighting in the Crusades. Although she was a member of the Royal Family of Hungary, she never missed a chance to share her wealth with others in need. She arranged for the poor to be given food at the castle gates and built a hospital where she volunteered as a nurse.

There were a few problems, however. Although Louis loved her dearly, it seems his relatives never liked her. After his death, those same in-laws forced her off the throne and out of the royal residence. Elizabeth and her children were left homeless and almost penniless.

Her faith and trust in God grew during those hard times. It's said that St. Francis of Assisi heard about the saintly ex-princess who was kind and loving in the face of hardship, and personally wrote to her about his newly-founded Third Order for lay people. Elizabeth was overjoyed at the chance to sign up, seeing membership as a great way to serve the poor and needy around her.

Elizabeth was eventually restored to her rightful position at court. After making sure her children were educated and provided for, she spent the last years of her life nursing the sick at that hospital she had founded with Louis. St. Elizabeth of Hungary also has the honor of being considered the patron saint of nurses.

It does seem like a fairytale: the happy ending of a wife-mother-princess-nurse-saint. But it really happened, and after a period of trial and tribulation, St. Elizabeth really did live happily ever after. And by investing in a little faith and hope and love, may the same be said about each one of us.

JOHN OF DAMASCUS
DECEMBER 4

St. John was the son of a Christian official at the court of the Khalif Abdul Malek in Damascus. When his father died, John inherited his civil service job. The Moslem leaders at the time (700 A.D.) had a good relationship with both Christians and Jews, and promoted them to high positions in the government. Charles appears to have been very happy at his job for several years, but then he had a sudden desire to change careers. Both John and his half-brother, Cosmos (who also became a saint) went off and joined a monastery.

John became famous as a great writer of hymns as well as theology books. One of his major writings was in defense of the use of icons (religious paintings, mosaics, etc.). There was a major fight in the Church at that time between the Iconoclasts (image-breakers) and the Iconodules (image-respecters). Iconoclasts held that the use of all religious images was a violation of the Second Commandment ("Thou shalt not make any graven image..."). The Iconodules' position, supported by St. John, was that the coming of Christ changed the interpretation of that commandment, since God, by taking human form in the person of Jesus, had blessed all human endeavors in His service, which would include painting, sculpture, music, and the spoken word. St. John also ran into trouble with some of his monk superiors for writing hymns. Some thought only the Psalms in the Bible were worthy to be sung in choir, not anything new.

The use of statues and other images in a church context has obviously been open to abuse throughout the ages, where people got lost venerating the item instead of what the item represents. In the 16th century some (but not all) of the early Protestants reacted by denouncing the use of images all together. No statues, no pictures, no stained-glass, no pictorial vestments, zero tolerance, if you will. It's not likely that the average person today would confuse a statue of Christ or one of the saints with reality and worship that statue...although if you visit certain old-fashioned churches in Europe, you might see evidence of things getting out of hand.

Our stained-glass windows at St. James' Episcopal Church in South Pasadena are a beautiful tool in learning about the life of Christ, just like the Bible or the Book of Common Prayer. Even the whole tradition of setting up a Nativity scene of little figures of the Holy Family, shepherds, angels, and Wise Men was first started by none other than St. Francis of Assisi to teach the common people what the Incarnation was all about. So in keeping with that Franciscan tradition, I always set up a good-sized Nativity Crèche on the altar in our Children's Chapel throughout the Advent and Christmas season.

I like to think of it as a medieval model railroad set. It's not some supernatural collection of mystical images, but a scenic depiction of the joy and wonder of a special Child being born in a special place and time, who continues to bring us the hope of a better world of peace on earth, good will toward men. I'm sure St. John would approve.

NICHOLAS
DECEMBER 6

St. Nicholas lived in what is now present-day Turkey around 300 A.D. He became a priest and was chosen as Bishop of the city of Myra at a relatively young age because of his education and good deeds. We do know he was listed as having attended the Council of Nicea and was a keynote speaker during the debates. He was well known in his time for his kindness and generosity, especially to the poor.

One day Nicholas heard of a family of three young girls and their father who were very poor and had no money for the girls' dowries, effectively preventing them from ever getting married to guys with good family connections. Bishop Nicholas went by their house at night in secret and dropped gold coins through the window. The coins supposedly fell into the girls' stockings which were hung up by their beds, and this is supposedly where we got the custom of hanging up stockings on Christmas Eve. At any event, St. Nicholas was linked to the idea of gift-giving, and in many countries in Europe, such as Holland and Spain, children still leave out their shoes on his feastday to be filled with little presents...or sticks if they've been bad. If fact our "Santa Claus" actually comes from the Dutch phrase "Sinter Klaas," which is an abbreviated form of "Saint Ni-cho-las."

Until I started doing research, I never realized that St. Nicholas was actually one of the most popular saints during the Middle Ages. The record shows that more churches were named after him during that time than after all the Apostles. Because of this public relations feat, Good St. Nicholas became the patron saint of children, sailors, farmers, bakers, and pawnbrokers.

Then how did we go from a sainted bishop to a red-suited Santa to symbolize the season? A big part of it comes from American advertising over the years, starting with Thomas Nast's Santa Claus cartoons from the Victorian era. And as people became uncomfortable about religion in the marketplace (and talking about saints seemed a little too religious for the average American in the 1800's), the saint faded out and the "right jolly old elf" faded into the picture. Our Santa Claus does represent the spirit of giving, but he's more along the lines of a Disney character: a nice, happy guy we all know and love, but not exactly someone with a proven track record of Christian service.

Which brings us back to our commemoration of St. Nicholas in the church year. In the midst of the holiday season with all its commercials and shopping and excitement, it's good to take a few minutes to remember that love and joy don't magically appear for ourselves and others. It takes personal initiative, and just doesn't happen unless we, like the real St. Nicholas, personally step in and reach out to others. So, yes, Virginia, there is a Santa Claus, and he's actually a saint!

Thomas the Apostle
December 21

The New Testament doesn't give us too much background information about St. Thomas. We know that he was Jewish and probably a Galilean by birth, but it's not mentioned what his occupation was before Christ gave him the job of apostle. Legends say he might have been an architect or builder, and that he later became a missionary to Persia and India.

Even though he was one of Christ's hand-chosen apostles, Thomas still had his share of problems and doubts, just like the rest of us. The only difference is that his doubts have been recorded for all posterity. Even his name is associated with someone who questions everything: a Doubting Thomas. "Unless I see the Risen Christ with my own eyes, I won't believe it."

But Thomas deserves better. Most of us forget that when Jesus was taking His final journey to Jerusalem, the other apostles tried to make Him change His mind for fear that the Jewish leaders might try to stone Him. Thomas was the only one who said, "Let us also go, that we may die with Him," clearly demonstrating how much he loved the Master at that moment in time.

We all have misgivings and uncertainties about life, our careers ...maybe even about ourselves. "What if I'm not good enough? What if nobody likes me? What if God can't forgive me for the horrible things in my past?"

St. Thomas had doubts about the future. It was Christ who healed him of his doubts and fears, and Christ will always do the same for each one of us. All we need is a little faith, a little hope, and a lot of love.